THE BOOK OF
RHYME&
REASON

THE BOOK OF
RHYME&
REASON
HIP-HOP 1994–1997

PETER SPIRER
FOREWORD BY ICE-T

REEL ART PRESS

Grandmaster Flash, Kurtis Blow and them passed the torch to us. Us and Run-DMC. LL Cool J, had it and passed it on to Rakim, Public Enemy, Boogie Down Productions. They took it on, passed it on. Who's getting it, you got EPMD coming out. Then you got your A Tribe Called Quest coming out. And then the West Coast caught some at the same time. They catching it with Ice-T, he caught part of it. He's running it now. The torch it going on to the next one and going on.

JALIL, WHODINI

FOREWORD

When *Rhyme & Reason* came out in 1997, it was very early in the game. Sure, I'd been successful to that point, but I hadn't even started on *Law & Order: Special Victims Unit*. Dr. Dre wasn't a mogul. Neither was Ice Cube.

So much has changed since then. At the time, it was expensive to make one song. Now, it's free. Back in the day, you had to make a demo. You had to actually make a tape to get what we call the "demo budget," where the label would give you enough money to go into the studio and it could cost $2,000 or $3,000 to make a song. Now, pretty much anybody with a laptop can make a record, make an album. They can make an album cover, get a barcode, and upload their music to a site. They really don't even need a laptop. With a phone, the technology is embedded to where people can actually make music if they know what they're doing. They don't even need a record label anymore. The record deal was a loan to allow you to make this record, and now you don't need that loan.

Since *Rhyme & Reason* was released, Hip-Hop just exploded. The culture let everybody know that no matter where you come from, you can actually do anything you want. I remember it was a big thing that a rapper would try to act. Now, rappers can own a record company. I don't just mean a record label, either. Rappers have clothing lines, film companies, television production companies. Now, a lot of us have cemented ourselves into the culture. I've been on television since the 1990s and am now the longest-running male actor in a TV series thanks to my role as Sergeant Odafin "Fin" Tutuola on *Law & Order: SVU*. I'm selling Cheerios, too. Dre is outta here with all his heavyweight production. Cube owns a basketball league. Snoop Dogg is selling pancakes.

The explosion has carried over to the other elements of Hip-Hop, too. Graffiti artists have blown up and have gone on to do fine art. The people that founded the small clothing lines like FUBU and Cross Colours have expanded into high fashion and other businesses.

All of this is possible because Hip-Hop opened the door to the idea of free enterprise for kids that were in the ghetto and thought all they could do was sell drugs, or be in gangs. Today, if you told anybody that anyone from Hip-Hop was doing anything, they'd believe it. "They're selling bicycles." "Okay, cool." "What are they doing?" "Oh, they've got an umbrella company." "Okay, that's cool." Hip-Hop just exploded in every direction. So, *Rhyme & Reason* was really just seeing us at our earliest stage.

Anytime you document something, which is what *Rhyme & Reason* did in 1997, you're trying to capture that moment. There's the theory that just because you're successful that you're gonna live forever. That couldn't be further from the truth. If you're successful, you have a higher chance of dying earlier because of excess. You have access to all these different opportunities and you really don't have people around you to tell you no. A lot of things can happen. Heavy D, Craig Mack, and The Notorious B.I.G. were in *Rhyme & Reason*. They've all passed since then. It isn't just rappers, either. No one could have ever imagined Kobe Bryant would be dead at 41. We're all human.

But thankfully, Hip-Hop lives on. Now we're at the genre's 50th anniversary, so Hip-Hop has gray hair. You can talk to a guy walking down the street with a cane and he'll be like, "I used to be a breakdancer" – and he's telling the truth. So, what was a youth movement is now fully mature. The first- and second-generation b-boys are now in their fifties. *Rhyme & Reason* is one of the few films that was there to document us before Hip-Hop truly exploded. I'm glad I was part of it.

Ice-T, November 2022, *as told to Soren Baker*

8

INTRODUCTION

As a film student at the University of Miami, I naturally studied photography. Though I was complimented for having a good eye by my professors, I was never satisfied with my photos. My photographs did not resemble those that I admired by other photographers. At the time I shot everything in 35mm.

A few years later I shot and directed a film about photographer Sally Mann. Watching Sally work with a large format camera I realized it wasn't my ability as a photographer that was the problem, it was the format in which I was shooting. After working with Sally, I purchased an old early '60s Twin Rolleiflex camera with an 80mm f2.8 Zeiss Planar lens. Shooting my first roll was eye opening. With its much bigger negative, my photos now had the qualities I was looking for: shallow depth

of field, sharp edges, and wonderful definition. I became inspired to photograph again. The timing was perfect.

My sister Danna introduced me to my partner and fellow producer for *Rhyme & Reason*, Chuck Block. I pitched Chuck the idea of doing a documentary. I told him that although I had worked on a number of music videos, I felt Hip-Hop had not been properly captured on film. Music videos at that time were perpetuating an ideal that was largely a myth and not true to life. While these videos were portraying an over-the-top lifestyle, the mainstream media was condemning Hip-Hop for being misogynistic and violent.

I had always found what was happening behind the camera of music videos more interesting. The dynamic

From left to right: Peter Spirer talking with The Notorius B.I.G. in his Manhattan apartment; with Hip-Hop pioneer and *Rhyme & Reason* co-producer Kurtis Blow; with Slick Rick; a Gold record of the soundtrack, awarded for over 500,000 copies sold.

between the artists and the relationships with people with whom they grew up was revealing. There is a fierce loyalty in Hip-Hop. Most artists feel an obligation to help bring up the people around them. When a rock band makes it, you don't see their friends go along for the ride or get a taste of the pie. Hip-Hop was different.

I wanted America to have a chance to see the human side of the culture and the people in it. The relationships of artists and their families, friends, and parents. I wanted to lower the volume so that we could hear from the artist and get their unfiltered thoughts about life, the biz, their hopes and dreams, and get a real peek into their world. I also wanted to create awareness for this amazing culture and create a historical record of what Hip-Hop was all about.

Rhyme & Reason was my second film. I decided along with my duties as a director/producer and sometimes cinematographer, I would also shoot with my Rollei. The great thing about the Rollei is that you get twelve pictures per roll. You have to be selective and discerning. It makes you slow down time. The waist level viewfinder also makes it an oddity. I had more than one artist ask, "What the f**k is that?" It looked like a relic from the past. It was, but they got it right when they made the Rollei.

The Rollei allowed me to capture some amazing moments: Puffy getting a trim in his office while doing three tasks at once; Biggie opening record plaques on his couch; Ice-T and Mack 10 hanging with their homies; Heavy D at the barber, playing pool, then celebrating at his "Nuttin' But Love" picnic. There was the "Jack The Rapper" convention with Death Row making a statement, all at a Disney World Hotel, that ended in chaos. There were magical moments such as Redman and Erick Sermon freestyling on the mic to amazed onlookers at a block party in Newark and watching Wu-Tang Clan chop it up on the block in Staten Island on a cold winter's day before they exploded.

In the '90s biting was a crime (if you don't know what that means, look it up). That's one of the things I loved about the culture. Every artist had their own unique style and flow, whether you were a DJ, MC, breaker, graffiti artist, beatboxer. I guess at the end of the day I wanted to make a film for anyone who's at a traffic light and gets intimidated by another car pulling up with a

fat soundsystem. I wanted to give an understanding of where that was coming from and what it was all about.

I documented what some refer to as the golden age of Hip-Hop. I've had these photographs for a long time. Many of which you are seeing for the first time.

When I first connected with the publisher of this book, Tony Nourmand, he asked me how many pictures I had. I replied, "I don't know." He said, "Well, is it 20 or 30 or a hundred?" "Honestly, I don't know," I said. Tony told me he was coming to Los Angeles and that he would take a look at what I had. I unearthed all the photographs and contact sheets from under my house where I had been keeping them and laid them

all out on my dining room table. When Tony arrived, he couldn't believe it, saying, "In my 30 years of doing this, whenever a photographer is vague about how much stuff he has, he always has very little or tons of garbage. You are the first person that has exceeded my expectations." Yeah, I shot a lot.

Perhaps my hesitation with looking back has to do with the pain of how many people have left us since making *Rhyme & Reason*. It's a crime to think of all the talented people we have lost. *Rhyme & Reason* was a dream come true and nightmare all rolled up into one. I have way too many war stories to share here. Like many other filmmakers, I felt like I was steamrolled over at times by the studio, Miramax. However, they put a

lot of resources behind the film and did get it onto the big screen. It paved the way for me to make more films.

I'm thankful that I had the foresight with my incredible team to document this culture and the wherewithal to take these photographs so that we have this record of this earth-shattering culture called Hip-Hop!

Peace,

D. Spirer

Peter Spirer, November 2022

From left to right: with Erick Sermon; shooting at the "Nuttin' But Love" cookout; working through a scene with Chuck D; a lighting test with Craig Mack in his New York kitchen

Key art for *Rhyme & Reason*

ENTER THE CHAMBER

"Rap is something that's being done. Hip-Hop is something that is being lived. A rap artist can be anybody from anywhere, but you got to visit the Bronx, period! Look at the projects, look at the people, see the environment that Hip-Hop started in."

17

KRS-ONE

1965 / BROOKLYN, NY

KRS-One (Knowledge Reigns Supreme Over Nearly Everyone) has been a significant figure in Hip-Hop since the mid 1980s, when he first emerged with Boogie Down Productions. He is considered one of the greatest rappers in the genre's history. One of the few artists to emphasize social and political issues, KRS-One also started the Stop the Violence movement. He remains creatively and politically active today.

KRS-ONE

"BETWEEN '75 AND '85, YOU HAD TO HAVE JUICE. YOU HAD TO HAVE POLITICAL POWER IN THE CULTURE OF HIP-HOP TO GRAB THE MIC, TO STEP OUT ONTO THE CARDBOARD AND BREAKDANCE. OR EVEN DO A PIECE. YOU HAD TO BE KNOWN IN THE COMMUNITY."

KRS-ONE

"I go to my own little world. I just express myself through breakin'. I dance, you know, I just get creative and I'm spinning and I feel like I'm flying. I'm flying in the air man, and I'm just free."

LIL' CEASE

"AND BACK AT THAT TIME, IN THE PIONEERING DAYS, IT WASN'T ABOUT MONEY. NO ONE CAME OUT TO GET PAID. WE USED TO SPEND MORE MONEY THAN WE MADE TO COME OUT AND PLAY. IT WAS A LOT OF HARD WORK TO BRING ALL THOSE SPEAKERS AND EQUIPMENT OUT, BUT WE JUST DID IT FOR THE LOVE OF HIP-HOP, JUST TO PLAY MUSIC."

24

GRANDMASTER CAZ

"This is where it all began pretty much.
The Godfather of Hip-Hop, Kool Herc, used to live right here."

GRANDMASTER CAZ

"Hip-Hop is the voice of this generation. Even if you didn't grow up in the Bronx in the '70s, Hip-Hop is there for you. It has become a powerful force. Hip-Hop binds all of these people, all of these nationalities, all over the world, together."

28
DJ KOOL HERC

1955 / KINGSTON, JA

The "father of Hip-Hop," DJ Kool Herc is said to have originated the genre at the fabled "Back to School Jam" for his sister on August 11, 1973 at 1520 Sedgwick Avenue, the Bronx; and then at subsequent parties throughout the decade. Using his groundbreaking "Merry-Go-Round" technique, he emphasised the breaks in the music. His friend, Coke La Rock, MC'd, speaking over the music in the Jamaican toasting tradition.

DJ KOOL HERC

"It was like radio shock waves with new styles of scratching and stuff. It's one of the original instruments of Hip-Hop. Us DJs would like go nuts, trying to learn those cuts."

SPEECH

"A really important part of Hip-Hop, I say, is Mike and Dave from the Crash Crew and Afrika Bambaataa. He brought, like, unity to people from the Bronx and Manhattan, brought them together."

34
BIZ MARKIE

1964–2021   /   EGG HARBOR TOWNSHIP, NJ

"The clown prince of Hip-Hop" was a pioneer; a singular and influential talent renowned for the wit and unique creativity that infused his beatboxing and rapping. He rose to prominence in Long Island house parties and through DJing in Manhattan, releasing his debut single, the Marl-produced "Make the Music With Your Mouth, Biz" in 1987. His most famous single, "Just a Friend," was released three years later.

"THE ROOFTOP WAS A CLUB UPTOWN THAT EVERYBODY'D GO, FROM THE HUSTLERS TO THE STRUGGLERS."

BIZ MARKIE

BIZ MARKIE

BIZ MARKIE

Examples from Biz Markie's collection of flyers documenting the birth of a culture, including the classic battle of all time, "Coldcrush Brothers vs Fantastic 5."

MR. FREEZE

KOOL DJ RED ALERT

"Grafitti is one of the most beautiful artforms in the world, you know ... them brothers grafittiing they're giving you first hand what they're seeing every day in the hood. They're bringing the news to you."

WISE INTELLIGENT

"Political rap and conscious rap tried to make people look what they was doing. and if they were doing things in a negative way. tried to look at it in an unhip way. tried to make it unhip and unfashionable."

46
CHUCK D

1960 / LONG ISLAND, NY

A giant of Hip-Hop with a long and storied career, Chuck D formed Public Enemy with Flavor Flav in 1985. With their socially-conscious and politically-charged lyrics, they are considered one of the most influential groups in Hip-Hop history. Their debut LP, *Yo! Bum Rush the Show*, was one of the fastest-selling rap records of all time; their second, *It Takes a Nation of Millions to Hold Us Back*, is one of the most significant albums of the twentieth century.

"EDUCATION IS KEY 'CAUSE IT TELLS PEOPLE WHAT TO LOOK OUT FOR AND HOW TO PREPARE THEMSELVES."

CHUCK D

"I've been thinking about going back to school because, I mean, my knowledge is limited right now. Everything I know, everything I deal with is limited. I'm not a big drug dealer with 25 years on my head. I sing rap records and I can make my bread. I'm not a doctor or a lawyer, but I'm 21 with a start."

51
NAS

1973 / BROOKLYN, NY

East Coast rapper Nas released his debut album, *Illmatic*, in 1994. A vivid, beat-poet observation of life on the streets in Queens, the album is a critically-acclaimed masterpiece and a cornerstone of the Hip-Hop genre.

Nas worked with multiple legendary producers on *Illmatic*, including Large Professor, Pete Rock, Q-Tip and DJ Premier. The album also featured guest appearances from, among others, Nas's father, jazz musician Olu Dara.

"After growing up here and seeing my man that lived upstairs get killed, and then my brother shot, like that showed me what type of world this shit is. The most time I feared living here, when I was young and I couldn't defend myself from shit that was going on, 'cause it was older niggas doing shit. It was a big world and I was young and all I had was my mom and my brother, you know."

NAS (WITH JUNGLE & WIZ, L-R)

"IT FEEL LIKE WHEN COPS COME OUT HERE, THEY COME FOR ONE THING AND ONE THING ONLY, AND THAT'S TO SHOOT YOU. LIKE WE WERE BORN TO BE WRONG, AND THEY COME JUST TO REGULATE US. YOU COULD BE A DOCTOR ON YOUR DAY OFF, CHILLIN' IN YOUR LUXURY CAR AND THE COPS PULL YOU OVER. THERE'S NO TELLIN' WHAT'S GONNA HAPPEN WHEN THE SIREN GO OFF."

NAS

"Violence is part of that lifestyle. You have to rap about it. If the kid is in a gang, then he raps from the perspective of a gang banger. What if the kid sells drugs? He is rapping from the perspective of a drug dealer. What if the guy's a pimp? He'll rap the perspective of a pimp."

ICE-T

1958 / NEWARK, NJ

Rapper, producer and actor, Ice-T first rose to prominence with his song "Reckless," on the soundtrack for the film *Breakin'* (1984). In 1986, he released "6 'N The Morning," one of the first gangsta rap records, and a year later, he released his debut album, *Rhyme Pays*. He also performed the title track for the movie *Colors* (1988) about LA gang life. The success of the album and film made him one of the first West Coast rappers to achieve national fame.

"I WOULD RAP ABOUT TRYING TO PARTY BUT MY BOYS WERE SAYIN' 'ICE MAN, WHY YOU RAP ABOUT PARTIES? WE ROB PARTIES MAN.'"

ICE-T

ICE-T

"That is where white America pisses me off. Arnold Schwarzenegger can blow away an entire police force in his movie, but Mack 10 talks about shooting one cop they want to ban his records ... that's hard for you to swallow."

MACK 10

"EVEN WITH ALL OF THE SUCCESS AND PROGRESS THAT HIP-HOP HAS MADE THROUGHOUT THE LAST 20 YEARS, IT HAS BEEN, YOU KNOW, WITH SOME GREAT COST. LIVES HAVE BEEN LOST, CAREERS HAVE BEEN FORGOTTEN."

66

EXPRESS STOP
305 TROPICAL FRUITS PRODUCTS - COLD DRINKS - VEGETABLES
EXPRESS
WHEN MY HEART CAN
BEAT NO MORE..
I HOPE I DIE FOR A
PRINCIPAL THAT I
HAVE LIVED FOR..
I WILL DIE BEFORE
MY TIME BECAUSE
I ALREADY
THE SHADOWS DEPTH
SO MUCH I WANTED TO
ACCOMPLISH BEFORE
I REACHED MY DEATH
I HAVE COME TO GRIPS
WITH THE POSSIBILITY
AND WIPED THE LAST
TEAR FROM MY EYES
OF MY DEMISE..
TUPAC 1992
MAKEVELI

"The same crime element that white people are scared of, black people are scared of. While they waiting for legislation to pass and everything, we next door to the killer. **We next door to them!**

We up in the projects, 80 niggas in the building. All them killers they letting out they right there in that building. But it's better. Just 'cause we black we get along with the killers or something? We get along with the rapist 'cause we black and we from the same hood? What is that? We need protection too."

TUPAC SHAKUR

"I GOT SHOT. I WAS CONFINED TO A WHEELCHAIR FOR LIKE A YEAR AND A HALF. I WAS SHOT NINE TIMES, YOU KNOW. THAT AIN'T NO SURPRISING THING ... IT HAPPENS IN EVERY GHETTO. SOMEBODY GETS SHOT, KILLED EVERYDAY."

70

POSDNUOS

"I don't care who you are, fuck it. You them niggas playing all that hardcore shit, stop it 'cause y'all niggas have kissed your mama before man. Y'all niggas have been in vulnerable states where y'all niggas have cried. Ain't none of y'all niggas out there iron man. You know what I am saying. If you say that, you're lying. I have faith that people are gonna wake up man. I really do. I have that faith."

Q-TIP

"My cousin, he was hired as a bodyguard, and eventually started wantin' to force money from me almost like a type of extortion thing ... At the time I was young, and I was thinkin' street law or whatever the case, take the law into my own hands."

74

SLICK RICK

1965 LONDON, UK

One of Hip-Hop's eminent lyrical storytellers, Slick Rick was part of Doug E. Fresh & the Get Fresh Crew in the mid 1980s. Their songs "The Show" and "La Di Da Di" are classics of the genre and the latter is one of the most sampled songs in history. In 1986, Slick Rick became the third artist signed to Def Jam Records and in 1988, he released his hugely influential debut album, *The Great Adventures of Slick Rick*.

"At the time I wasn't thinking, I didn't think I had a choice. At the time, I'm thinking this individual is out to get me, this individual is havin' people try to kill me that I don't know, and I felt my back was against the wall and I felt that what I was doin' was the right thing. You know, after you sit in jail you realize what you could do, you know? Like maybe bringing it to the law's attention, and movin' until the situation is handled, or whatever the case, but at the time, when you in it, you don't, at that time anyway, I wasn't thinking like that, I was thinking something else ...

JAY-Z

"BLACK OWNED LABELS AREN'T BEING INTIMIDATED ANYMORE. YOU KNOW RUSSELL SIMMONS HAS ALWAYS BEEN OUT THERE WITH DEF JAM, AND SEAN 'PUFFY' COMBS WITH BAD BOY ENTERTAINMENT. THEY'RE ALL DOING THEIR THING."

KURTIS BLOW

"She was just a single black mother, and she gave me, you know, she didn't let nothing, no obstacles stand in her way. She overcame every obstacle. My mother owns my company. She owns Bad Boy. That was my gift to her. She was the only one that was always there for me no matter what."

82

SEAN "PUFFY" COMBS

1969 / HARLEM, NY

Rapper, producer, actor and entrepreneur, Sean "Puffy" Combs formed Bad Bay Entertainment in 1993, working closely with artists like Craig Mack, The Notorious B.I.G. and Faith Evans. Combs' "I'll Be Missing You," written as a tribute to Biggie after he was murdered in 1997, was the first rap song to debut at number one on the Billboard singles chart. It launched Combs' first album, *No Way Out*, to multi-platinum success.

SEAN "PUFFY" COMBS

"I don't give a fuck what nobody say. Ain't nobody get in this game to be an average motherfucker. Everybody that starts this shit they want to be the largest rapper in the world, and that's their dream. They wanna be LARGE. They wanna be in it."

86
THE NOTORIOUS B.I.G.

1972–1997 / BROOKLYN, NY

The Notorious B.I.G. was one of the most influential East Coast gangsta rappers of the 1990s. His 1994 record, *Ready to Die,* was critically acclaimed and a huge commercial success. Biggie was murdered in a drive-by shooting in 1997 at the age of 24. His second album, *Life After Death,* was released posthumously just two weeks after his death, selling over 10 million copies and reaching number one on the *Billboard 200.*

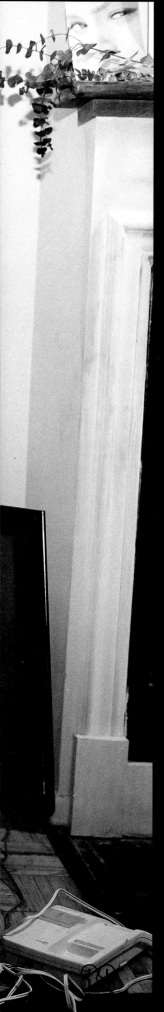

"I GOT MY PLATINUM JOINTS, 'BOUT TO POP THESE OUT. YOU KNOW NAH MEAN. BIG WILLY, FIRST BROOKLYN NIGGA TO GO PLATINUM. YOU KNOW, IT'S ALL GOOD IN THE HOOD. GOT MY GOLD JOINTS. JUICY OL' JOINTS. YOU KNOW. STRAIGHT OUTTA THE HOOD A NIGGA DID GOOD."

THE NOTORIOUS B.I.G.

"Everything happens for a reason. And I think me hustling, selling drugs, it schooled me to the streets a lot, you know. I learned a lot. I learned there's some things you can do and some things you can't do. Selling drugs to others is something you can't do. Just cannot do that. You will eventually die or go to jail. It's a fact."

THE NOTORIOUS B.I.G.

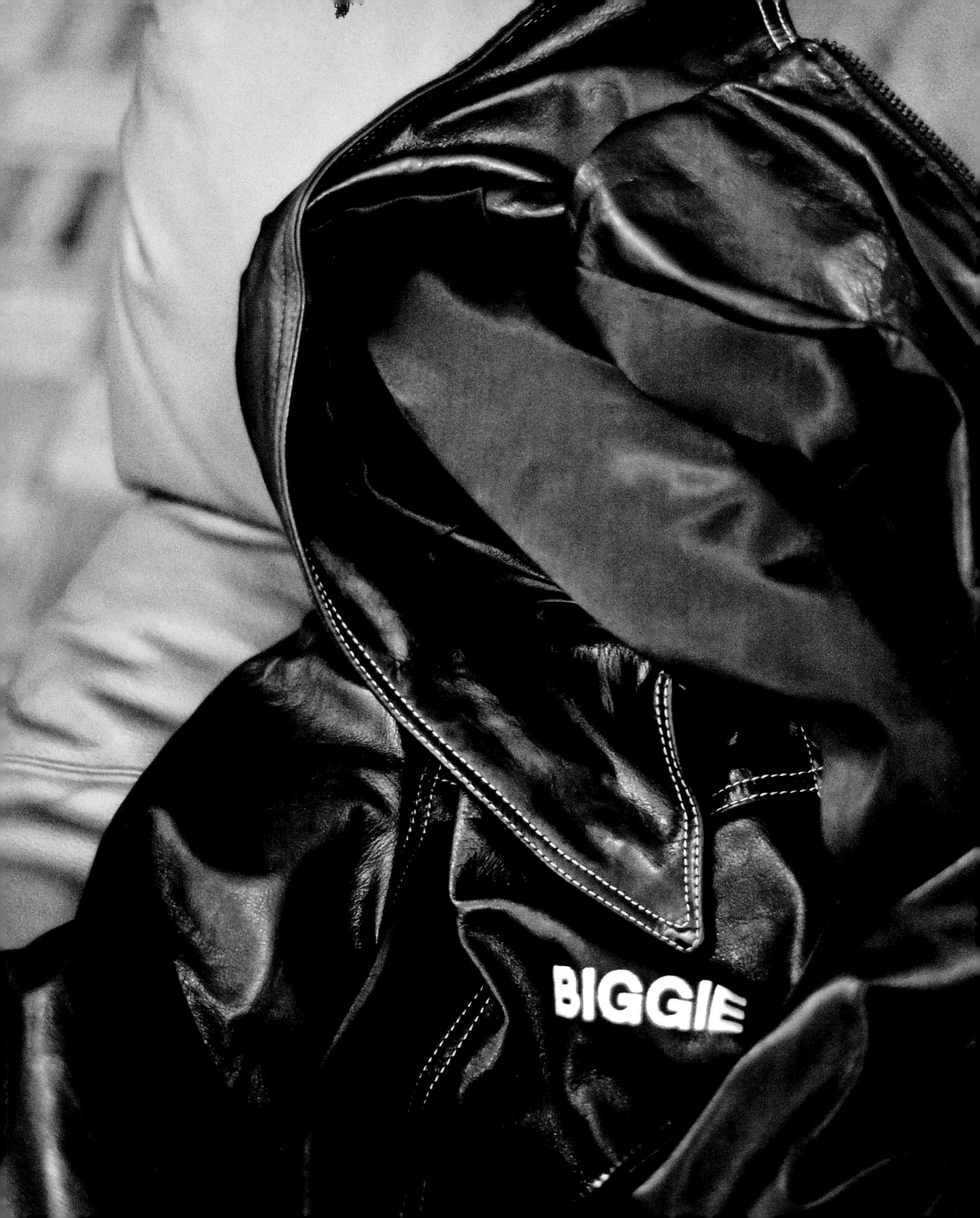
BIGGIE

"MY FIRST RECORD COMPANY ROBBED ME BLIND. I CAME FROM MAKING $20 A WEEK TO SOMEBODY WANTS TO GIVE ME $1000. I WAS LIKE, THIS IS CRAZY. BUT, THAT'S ALL I GOT."

"Inside the record industry you always have to stay conscious and in reality. You can never believe your own hype, 'cause those people will build you up to Superman, only to find out that you are Garbage man!"

WYCLEF JEAN

"You know you got the different slings, the Brooklyn slings, you got the West Coast, the down South, like the Goody Mobs an' all that. And it's a culture and we're all part of it."

PRAS

"Yeah I was hip to New York Hip-Hop. You got to give props when props is due. They originated it. Anybody that doesn't believe that is tripping. And they just spread it and now it's, um, bigger than ever. And it's going to get bigger."

97
DR. DRE

1965 / COMPTON, CA

Rapper, producer and businessman, Dr. Dre started out as a DJ and as part of World Class Wreckin' Cru in south-central LA. In 1986, he founded N.W.A. with Eazy-E and Ice Cube. Their debut album, *Straight Outta Compton* (1988), helped popularize gangsta rap. In 1992, Dre co-founded Death Row Records, producing multi-platinum albums with top artists, and also releasing his own best-selling album, *The Chronic* (1992).

"THE RECORD BUSINESS
IS EXACTLY WHAT IT IS,
RECORD. BUSINESS.
AND YOU HAVE TO TAKE
CARE OF BOTH."

DR. DRE

"I got into it just wantin' to make music, you know what I'm sayin'? I didn't really give a damn about the business part of it. I was trusting people, trusting that they would handle my business the way it was supposed to be handled, and you get fucked like that!"

DEATH ROW RECORDS AT *JACK THE RAPPER*, 1994

SEAN "PUFFY" COMBS WITH LUNIZ AT THE
POOL PARTY, *JACK THE RAPPER*, 1994

"When I go out West, I get so many fake gangsta groups, man. I mean chumps be like with mad pump shotguns on the cover. Yo! That shit be stupid. If you're livin' like that, you don't want anybody to see you with a picture like that, stupid."

GURU

"I REMEMBER WHEN BITING USED TO BE A CRIME. I MEAN, YOU KNOW HOW MANY BITES OF SNOOP THERE IS? SNOOP'S THE ORIGINAL. HE'S DOPE. THEN YOU GOT DAS EFX. WHEN THEY CAME OUT, EVERYBODY WANTED TO SOUND LIKE THEM. ONCE SOMEBODY COMES OUT AND DOES SOMETHING DOPE, LEAVE IT ALONE."

GURU

KRAZY DRAYZ, PARRISH
SMITH & SKOOB (L-R)

114

PARRISH SMITH

KRAZY DRAYZ

DAS EFX

"In the east. It's always on throat no teeth.
I'm the least concerned with how many niggas
you burned. I extinguish your flame. take gain
out your brain. have a nigga in pain. have
you walking with a cane. Money and fame you
got your fucking self to blame."

XZIBIT

DJ DICE

KING JUST

KING JUST

"We still keeping it real. As you see it's mad people out here, right here right now. That's just with us, cause this is how it's been before the rap shit even came off, you know what I'm saying. Therefore, you see our chamber. Niggas got beer, niggas is still watching their back from the cops. But it's all real."

RAEKWON

129
WU-TANG CLAN

1992 / STATEN ISLAND, NY

In the mid 1990s, Wu-Tang Clan's sound was one of the most recognizable and critically acclaimed in Hip-Hop. Formed in 1992 as a loose collection of nine MCs, their first single, "Protect Ya Neck," became an underground hit and gave them the cachet to negotiate a revolutionary record deal that still allowed each member to pursue a solo career. Collectively and individually, they have released eight studio albums and dozens of solo albums.

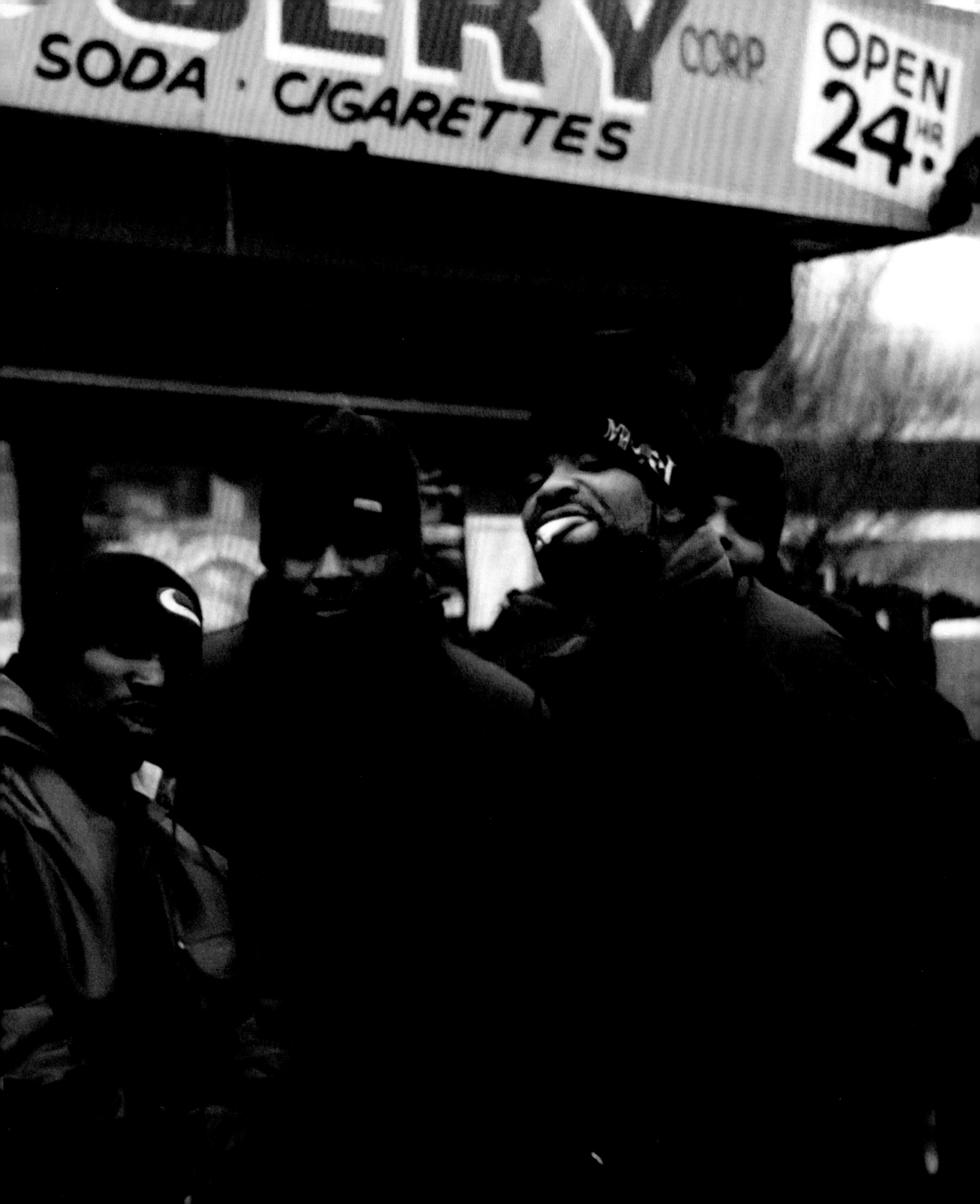
SODA · CIGARETTES
CORP
OPEN
24 HR

"HIP-HOP IS HOW YOU WALK, TALK, LIVE, DRESS, ACT, SEE, SMELL, FART, SHIT, FUCK, YOU KNOW WHAT I MEAN. IT'S ALL THAT RIGHT THERE."

134

RZA

"AS FAR AS MUSIC GO, YOU GOT YOUR WATERED DOWN NIGGAS, THEN YOU GOT YOUR HAPPY GO LUCKY NIGGAS, THEN YOU GOT YOUR HARD CORE NIGGAS, AND THE UNDERGROUND NIGGAS. BASICALLY, IT'S ALL DRUG BLOCKS. EVERYBODY SELLING THEIR DOPE ON THEIR BLOCK. WHAT WE SAYING TO Y'ALL IS LIKE THIS, WE GOT OUR SHIT SEWED UP, SO DON'T TRY TO COME ON OUR BLOCK SELLING YOUR SYNTHETIC SHIT 'CAUSE YOU GON' GET BLOWED UP."

METHOD MAN

ERICK SERMON, PARRISH SMITH

"Everybody in this motherfucker got a dark side to them. Some of you motherfuckers do something and you don't want me to know about it, right? But, on my album I'm doing it all and letting you know about it. You know what I'm saying? When you journey into my shit, you need flashlights. You want to enter my mind, you need flashlights. You want to enter my world, you need flashlights 'cause it's dark over here."

140   REDMAN

ERICK SERMON

"IT'S ALL YOUNG GUYS, FROM 27 ON DOWN, RUNNING THE SHIT ..."

PARRISH SMITH

"HIP-HOP IS AN ELEMENT THAT WAS CREATED BY THE YOUTH FROM THE STREET, YOU KNOW, AND WE GONNA CONTINUE EXPRESSING THAT TRUTH AND THAT YOUTHFUL EXPRESSION."

BUSTA RHYMES (WITH RAMPAGE, L-R)

148

"Performing is the shit for me as an artist 'cause this is where I get to penetrate the individual. This is how I get into the individual's mind, body and soul. I get to inspire the way they gonna feel. I think the energy is really inspired by the music and the people. Performing is everything."

BUSTA RHYMES

"Hip-Hop music is an expression of what you know. We try to express, like, the funny side, good side or normal side of the 'hood that people really don't talk about. We're always hearing about the negative but we're always trying to talk about the positive." DOITALL

150
L.O.T.U.G.
(LORDS OF THE UNDERGROUND)

1990-Present / Newark, NJ

With their politically-aware raps and hard beats, L.O.T.U.G. were a significant influence on 1990s Hip-Hop. Mr. Funke, DoItAll and Lord Jazz (l to r, opposite) released their debut album, Here Come the Lords, in 1993. Produced by Marley Marl and K-Def, it featured five charting singles, including "Chief Rocka," which reached number one on the rap charts that year. They are still together, writing music and touring worldwide.

DJ LORD JAZZ

MR. FUNKE

LORDS OF THE UNDERGROUND CREW

"YOU CAN NOT TAKE AWAY THIS NEGATIVE HIP-HOP EITHER, BECAUSE IT'S NOT REALLY THAT IT'S NEGATIVE, BUT THOSE BROTHERS ARE JUST SPEAKING ABOUT WHAT THEY KNOW."

156   DOITALL (WITH DJ LORD JAZZ)

"That's the fact of why I live here ... away from the fucked shit, because I didn't have that opportunity when I was a youth. I didn't have no choice ... I had nowhere else to go. I don't put my city down, I love Compton to the fullest, but with me being a grown man, me being a father, a businessman, owning a company and all that, me staying in Compton would mean me having to deal with the same situations as I dealt with as a teenager. And then I have to think about my kids growing up in the environment I grew up in, so I moved out. I send my kids to the good schools. I moved to a community where I can walk out my front door, and I wouldn't have to see gang writing and shit like that. Because I lived in that shit all my life, and I figured if you can move out you might as well, to better yourself and to better your future family."

MC EIHT

MC EIHT

SLIMKID3

"YEAH, I GOT A FATHER BUT HE AIN'T SHIT. HE WAS NEVER THERE. MY MOM AND MY GRANDMOTHERS RAISED ME. MY MOM HAD ANOTHER HUSBAND BUT I AIN'T CRAZY ABOUT HIM. HE A DRUNK. THAT'S PROBABLY THE REASON I DON'T DRINK, 'CAUSE THAT MOTHERFUCKER, HE STANK."

DA BRAT

JERMAINE DUPRI

"YOU TAKE A PHILLY OR A SWISHER – WHATEVER TASTES GOOD TO YOU. SPLIT DOWN THE MIDDLE, TAKE ALL THAT NICOTINE SHIT OUT, ALL THAT BROWN SHIT, OKAY. AND JUST FILL IT WITH WEED. BIG, AS FAT AS YOU WANT. SMALL AS YOU WANT. IF IT'S SOME BOMB ASS WEED IT DON'T NEED TO BE THAT FAT."

168

DA BRAT

"Shit ain't changing man, shit's getting worse out here if anything. That's just a part of everyday life, it ain't nuttin' shockin' or surprising us, it's just like the same old thing, see it everyday." DJ MUGGS

170
CYPRESS HILL

1988-Present / South Gate, CA

A defining influence on the development of West Coast rap and Hip-Hop, Cypress Hill have sold over 20 million albums worldwide. The Latin-American group, comprised of Sen Dog, B-Real and DJ Muggs (and later Eric "Bobo" Correa), were the first major Hip-Hop group to include Spanish slang in their lyrics and they have also openly pushed for the use of medical and recreational marijuana. All ten of their LPs are critically acclaimed.

"IN '85 THERE WAS A WEED DROUGHT, AND '86 WAS THE YEAR CRACK CAME IN, AND EVERYTHING CHANGED."

DJ MUGGS

"I SOLD IT AND I'VE SEEN WHAT IT DOES TO PEOPLE ... AND I KINDA GOT A BAD CONSCIOUS ABOUT IT."

B-REAL

"YOU GOTTA LISTEN TO THE SHIT. TO UNDERSTAND IT, REWIND IT THREE OR FOUR TIMES, LISTEN TO IT. THEN MAYBE YOU'LL GET A LITTLE NOTION FROM WHERE WE ARE COMING FROM."

176

SPICE 1

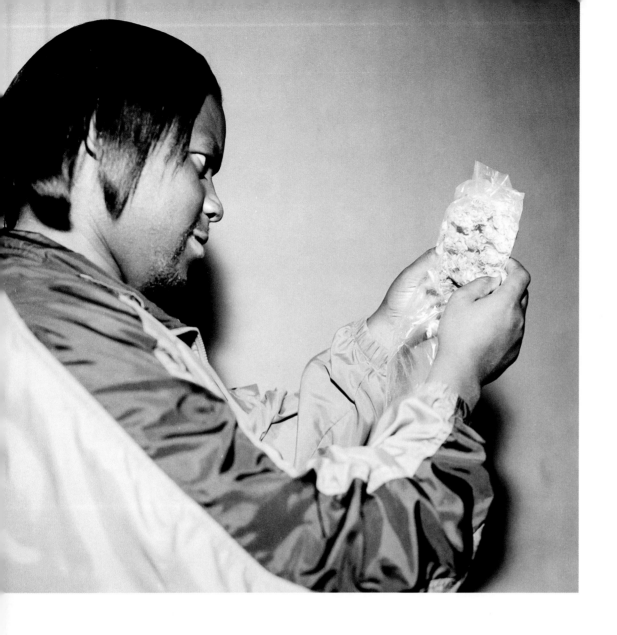

KRIS KROSS

DJ LET LOOSE

LUNIZ

"WE USED TO SELL TAPES AT GROCERY STORES, LIQUOR STORES, BARBER SHOPS, BEAUTY SALONS, TIRE SHOPS, WHATEVER, HOWEVER. LET IT' TAKE OFF FROM THERE."

188

"I get inspiration from my lifestyle and the people around me and my family. I'm grateful for all my blessings. I've gone through a lot of bad shit in my time but I've had more blessings than disappointments so I tend to smile in the face of God rather than frown in the face of God."

191
HEAVY D

1967–2011 / Mandeville, JA

One of the most charismatic, generous and popular Hip-Hop performers, Heavy D first emerged in 1987 with Heavy D & The Boyz. Their records were feel-good, infectious hits and they became the first act signed to Uptown Records. As a producer, Heavy D helped launch the careers of Sean "Puffy" Combs and The Notorious B.I.G. He also put on an annual "Nuttin' But Love" cookout in Mount Vernon, which drew large crowds.

"When I did that 'Nuttin' But Love' cookout I wanted it to be fun. we got together. it was just before summer. we were about to go on tour and we were like before we go on tour let's do something special. so I said alright. let's do something just for the community."

HEAVY D

Scenes from the first "Nuttin' But Love" annual cookout organized by Heavy D, which took place in his hometown of Mount Vernon, New York.

PLAY

LL COOL J

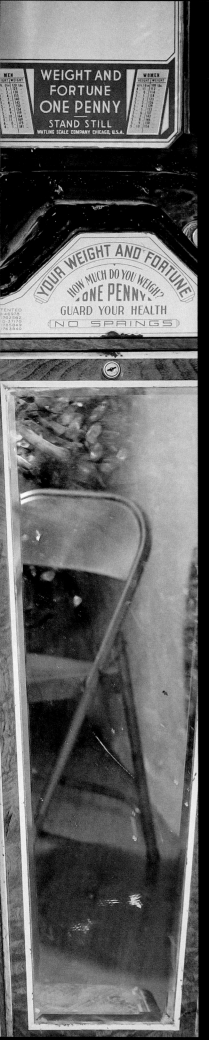

"THE STRUGGLES TODAY ARE DIFFERENT. IT'S NOT AS HARD AS IT USED TO BE WHEN WE STARTED TEN YEARS AGO. WHEN YOU HAD TO CONVINCE MUTHAFUCKERS THAT THIS SHIT SELLS. RAP SELLS."

HEAVY D

PAUL STEWART

(SALT) "We've been able to endure a lot of hard times because we do care about each other. But, um, she makes it fun. This girl is crazy. We've always found it our duty as female artists to tell the other side of the story. We are about telling the ladies to respect yourself, love yourself, (PEPA) and to tell the females not to give them so much to talk about."

THA GOVENER, ERICK SERMON,
DIEZZLE DON & REDMAN

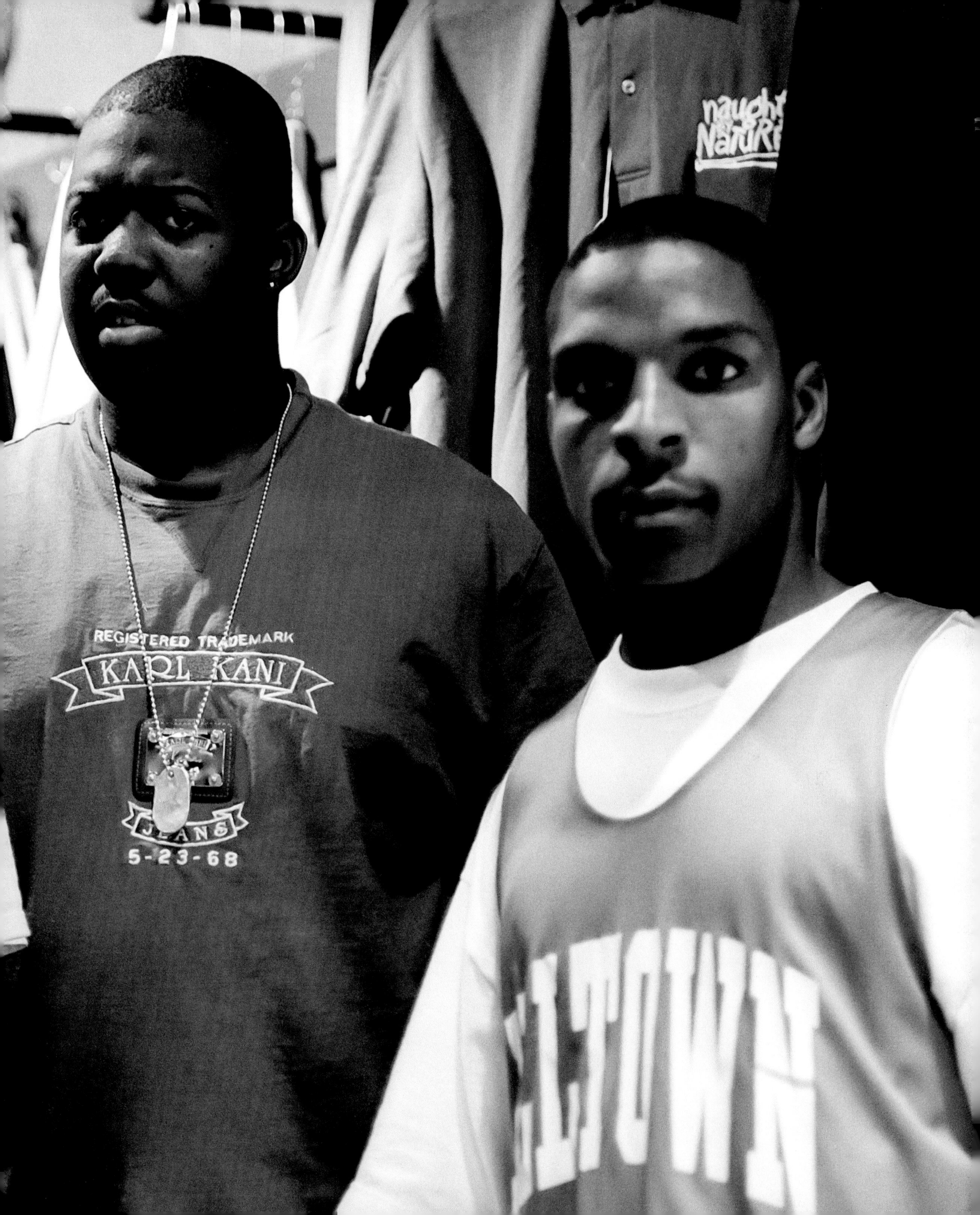
REGISTERED TRADEMARK
KARL KANI
JEANS
5-23-68

KEITH MURRAY

REDMAN

KAYGEE, TREACH

VIN ROCK

TREACH

KAYGEE (ABOVE)

"PEOPLE WHO'RE REPRESENTING THE ESTABLISHMENT, THEY'RE THREATENED BY HIP-HOP. THEY'RE THREATENED BY INTELLIGENT AND ARTICULATE BLACK PEOPLE WHO HAPPEN TO REPRESENT, THE POOR PEOPLE, YOU KNOW WHAT I MEAN, THE HAVE NOTS."

LAURYN HILL (WITH KURTIS BLOW)

"I KNOW THAT HIP-HOP IS THE REPRESENTATION OF THIS OPPRESSED CULTURE, AND I WILL REPRESENT THAT 'TIL THE DAY I DIE."

KRS-ONE

produced by
Charles X Block
Peter Spirer
and
Daniel Sollinger

executive in charge of production
Shannon McIntosh

230
INSIGHTS

When I first met Peter in 1992, he told me about an idea he had for a Hip-Hop documentary, and we embarked on a five-year journey to make *Rhyme & Reason* a reality. Our big break came when we met Diezzle Don. Diezzle Don & Tha Govener arranged a guided tour of Newark. We visited the Naughty Gear store, ending with a block party with hundreds of people, attended by Redman, Craig Mack and Erick Sermon all freestyling. Another important shoot was at the Jack the Rapper convention. Adario Strange from *The Source* and Hip-Hop legend DJ Kool Herc accompanied us and it provided a bonanza of footage: Redman and Keith Murray freestyling; Puffy Combs handing out T-shirts; pool parties; and culminating in pandemonium. While filming over 80 Hip-Hop artists nationwide, Peter brought his Rolleiflex Twin f2.8 Planar camera with him. These photos documented a critical time in the evolution of Hip-Hop.
CHARLES X BLOCK – PRODUCER

I worked on many of the early music videos in Hip-Hop (A Tribe Called Quest, Fresh Prince, etc). At the time, there were little to no documentaries about Hip-Hop. When Peter asked me to help produce *Rhyme & Reason* I jumped at the chance. I knew we would get full support from the artists, because they wanted their culture and their lives to be documented. *Rhyme & Reason* stands as a time capsule of the golden age of Hip-Hop, full of innovation and expansion. Over the course of shooting, Hip-Hop moved from underground to mainstream, Tupac passed and Biggie passed the weekend of our premiere. *Rhyme & Reason* was a high watermark in my career as a film producer.
DANIEL SOLLINGER – PRODUCER

Long before the proliferation of the modern-day music documentary, there was *Rhyme & Reason*. A documentary with a "theatrical" release, no less. Working on this groundbreaking movie gave me the lifelong dream of being Busta Rhymes for a day! It was exhilarating but tiring to work the long days and nights sifting through hours and hours and hours (did I say hours?) of interviews and b-roll with Peter and the team. But Peter's vision paid off in the end and we were all so proud of the movie.

I remember the opening weekend like it was yesterday. Unfortunately our box office joy quickly turned to sorrow as we learned of the murder of The Notorious B.I.G. I am forever moved by his words and music, and my heart still breaks at a life lost so young. Thank you Peter for celebrating the world of Hip-Hop and rap in such an extraordinary way.
SHANNON McINTOSH – EXEC. IN CHARGE OF PRODUCTION

I remember working on *Rhyme & Reason* with Peter. It was fascinating being in front of the camera once again as well as, for the first time, contributing behind the scenes as an associate producer. From pre-production, talent acquisition, the various shot locations, recording the soundtrack and post, I experienced the world of film production like never before and fell in love. Thank you Peter for the opportunity. I have learned much from you and the rest of the team. However, it was bittersweet filming Biggie at the CNN building in Hollywood. RIP Big Poppa, Tupac and the rest of our fallen Hip-Hop soldiers!
KURTIS BLOW WALKER – ASSOCIATE PRODUCER

associate producers
Kurtis Blow
and
Danna Berentsen

co producer
Richard Spero

Spirer did an excellent job of curating both interviews and images for the film. Even more important, using a light touch to place them in context. 1997 was a chaotic and volatile time for both the art form and the business of Hip-Hop; with the murder of Biggie on one end of the spectrum and the long suppressed breakthrough of artists like Salt-N-Pepa, Dr. Dre, Jay-Z and Lauryn Hill on the other. The film captures that tension.

HELENA (PEREZ) ECHEGOYEN - MIRAMAX ACQUISITIONS

At the time, I had no idea I was meeting one of the giants of Hip-Hop. I was just thrilled to be working with my brother Peter! It was, like, 5 a.m. when we found the brownstone. As we were setting everything up for the interview, I heard footsteps get louder and louder. Biggie Smalls came into the room in his boxers. I quickly averted my gaze, but it was too late! Biggie shouted out, "I didn't know there'd be bitches here!" He put on some clothes, lit up a blunt and offered it to each of us. Peter declined, as did the two other guys on our crew. Biggie looked at Peter and said, "Don't none of you white motherf"**ers smoke?" Peter kind of gestured towards me, and with a big smile, Biggie handed me the blunt. Epic.

DANNA WEBB - ASSOCIATE PRODUCER

A chance encounter meeting Peter on a snowy winter day led to co-producing *Rhyme & Reason* and a lifelong friendship/ business partnership. While waiting to take off for hours on a flight from JFK back to LA, we happened to be seated right next to each other. We quickly became friends, talking about him coming out to LA for his Academy Award nomination

luncheon and me working at the William Morris Agency. Months later when he asked if I was interested in working on the West Coast shoot of his independent Hip-Hop film, it was an opportunity I couldn't pass up. Peter gave artists the opportunity to have a voice, share their stories, and explore culture, fashion, and music ... like audiences had never seen before. It was relatable and honest, with nothing held back. Being persistent was key, and eventually everybody wanted to be a part of it. So many great stories, but to me the best will always be that initial encounter on that flight back to LA.

RICHARD SPERO - CO-PRODUCER

I was an outsider to this culture, but Peter had an in. I was often winging it with the older 16mm cameras in marginal conditions, but I could tell we were on to something special. Magical insider moments were abundant: Peter whispering that this quiet 17-year-old kid who was protective of his mom's apartment in the projects was going to be big (Nas); the back office where Sean "Puffy" Combs was effortlessly dealing with five people's attention at once; Method Man spitting rhymes outdoors on a bitter cold day (then teaching me how a blunt gets rolled). The stills had to squeeze into crammed agendas, but seeing them now I'm reminded how special these times were, and how prescient Peter was taking those extra minutes!

SEAN ADAIR - EAST COAST CINEMATOGRAPHER

We were holed up in a small editing room just off the Sunset Strip at Crescent Heights. A lot of the rappers would stop by to see their parts in the film (yes it was shot on film) and I was

edited by
Andy Robertson
and
David Wilson

music supervisors
Happy Walters
and
Andrew Shack

ike a kid in the candy store watching them view the movie for the first time; Dr. Dre bumping his head in acknowledgment, Xzibit laughing his ass off as he watched himself. It was a great time in Hip-Hop history. Let's make the sequel!

DAVID WILSON – EDITOR

Rhyme & Reason embodied the DIY spirit of early Hip-Hop. Many scenes were filmed on 16mm short ends – smaller rolls of leftover stock that are re-sold at a deep discount. These short rolls of film meant that the camera needed to be reloaded more frequently and many shots end in roll-outs: big flares of reddish and orange light that occur if the last few feet gets exposed to sunlight as the camera is reloaded. We used these light flares to create the documentary's editorial style. The stylistic side-effects of using short ends are a cinematic expression of the Hip-Hop ethos.

ANDY ROBERTSON – EDITOR

The soundtrack to *Rhyme & Reason* features some of the greatest voices in Hip-Hop. The time was so distinct, and the music was rebellious and unabashedly honest. The artists were excited to have this movie made about the culture which showed it in such a real way. You could feel the energy – a celebration and a platform. I remember getting songs out of the studio and just having so many different thoughts on where they could land against picture. We spent hours, days, months trying to get it right. "Nothin' But the Cavi Hit" always got me as being so sticky. I also loved the clever flip on the end credit song "Reason for Rhyme" by 8Ball & MJG. *Rhyme & Reason* is from a time before every moment was recorded and we are lucky to have this testimony to history.

SPRING ASPERS – MUSIC SUPERVISOR

Rhyme & Reason has a special look and feel to it. Back then we didn't have many of the tools available today. Peter came up with the idea of shooting the stills using polarized lights. We spread out a group of photos on a wall, mixed in with press articles treated in Photoshop. The 16mm footage was then transferred to video and reshot on film again directly on a high definition monitor. This gave the graphic elements a distinctive texture. Not to mention the satisfaction of having collaborated on an incredible project that resonates even to this day.

FRANCISCO GIORGIO SFERRA – VISUAL CONSULTANT

None of us really had a ton of experience doing a doc and I think that's why the film came out so well. It was visceral, raw, and completely "of the moment." They say Hip-Hop is art music and culture flipped on its side and that's exactly what inspired me in making the title sequence. I really enjoyed the process: my Bolex 16mm movie camera, a Xerox machine and a cool font that Peter helped pick out. Creating purposeful light leaks, using broken and distressed film, playing with lens focal lengths, filming on opaque and transparent paper and film etc. I played Public Enemy's *Fear of a Black Planet* the entire shoot. There was no video playback, so it was fascinating seeing the results in the telecine. I think the style and look of the titles dovetails nicely with the Wu-Tang interview and Busta Rhymes live show intro.

KENAN MORAN – OPENING TITLE SEQUENCE

Working on *Rhyme & Reason* was my first job in LA, and such a remarkable introduction to the city for a naive white kid from Wisconsin. I talked to Dr. Dre on the phone on my first day! And then got to meet a who's who of the Hip-Hop community – in Compton and Lynwood, but also in Sacramento and the

Hollywood Hills. What strikes me most about the film some 25 years later is the intimate, easy-going rapport Peter found in his surprisingly vulnerable subjects: Sean "Puffy" Combs (not yet Puff Daddy) getting a haircut at his executive desk; Craig Mack washing dishes; Biggie Smalls coolly unwrapping Gold records like they were cough drops; and Nas opening his heart on a brownstone staircase. Then again, Tupac and Biggie were both then murdered and, in retrospect, one must confront the palpable end of a more innocent era: rap had suddenly crossed a threshold from subculture to capital "C" Culture, and *Rhyme & Reason* marks that transition as well as any other document of its time.

MICHAEL NED HOLTE - ASSISTANT TO THE DIRECTOR

clearly remember the day of the Ice-T shoot. We started out at his home in the Hollywood Hills with the infamous shark tank. Afterwards we continued on to his "office" with his crew. It was located in a storefront on LaBrea. I was struck by its austerity - it was dimly lit and modestly furnished; not at all what I was expecting from a world famous rapper. His crew was welcoming ... especially one who wanted my number, not realizing that I was with the director. He was young and attractive ... I didn't mind.

KELLY BEVAN - ASSOCIATE PRODUCER

was approached by my good friend Happy Walters to see if I wanted to do the soundtrack for *Rhyme & Reason*. It was a no brainer ... I walked into our A&R Marvin Watkins' office and said we need a banger and he and Mack 10 said we're going to try something with Tha Dogg Pound. My first thoughts were these rights will not be easy to get, how much is this going to cost and how will they sound together? We went to the studio and from

the first listen I was like, wow, this is a monster. Mack and Marvin came through and "Nothin' But the Cavi Hit" turned into a West Coast classic. Everyone was happy to support the film and give the rights needed. At that time Tha Dogg Pound was one of the biggest artists out there. The most important thing you need for a soundtrack is a single that actually works in the film and works to sell the album and hopefully at radio. We got all three.

ANDREW SHACK - EXEC. PRODUCER OF SOUNDTRACK

I felt very blessed to be a part of such an impactful film as *Rhyme & Reason*. Its timing is probably its most important attribute. It was filmed at a time of the existence but fastly fading innocence of the Hip-Hop community. This would be the last time a Hip-Hop documentary would be able to get so many icons of the industry to participate. It was still a time when even the stars were excited to be filmed and it captures this amazing moment when Hip-Hop was exploding beyond anyone's wildest dreams.

PAUL STEWART - CO-EXEC. PRODUCER OF SOUNDTRACK

I had the opportunity to work with Creative Cafe on the sound editing and music for the movie. Working with Dana Gustafson, Steve Flick, and Spring Aspers was a joy as we all had a common goal to help make this film legendary. I was familiar with some of the artists yet I learned so many stories behind the music. It was more than just about music, we were living it. The '90s were a special time and I got to see it fully documented in Peter's film. When Peter asked me to add my voice during the Tupac sequence I couldn't have been prouder. One of my most prized possessions is the Gold record soundtrack plaque for *Rhyme & Reason*. It doesn't get any more real than *Rhyme & Reason*.

DALE BROWN - SOUND EDITOR, VOICE OVER ARTIST

"RHYME & REASON" GIVES THANKS
TO ALL THE ARTISTS WHO
APPEAR IN THE FILM.

PEACE

236
ACKNOWLEDGMENTS

This book is dedicated to Sam and Rachel. My deepest thanks to my partner and producer on *Rhyme & Reason*, Chuck Block. Chuck, your enthusiasm and belief in what we were doing was an inspiration and allowed me the freedom to figure it out as we navigated from development to completion. My beautiful and talented sister, Danna Webb, who connected me with Chuck and helped in so many ways to make *Rhyme & Reason* a reality. Daniel Sollinger, who supported my vision and was a brother throughout the process. Richard Spero, who jumped in when we filmed in LA and added a boost when we needed it. All of our crew members and camera people, Sean Adair, Alex Rappoport and Antonio Arroyo. My two talented editors, David Wilson and Andy Robertson. Helena Echegoyen, for recognizing the significance of what we were doing. Shannon McIntosh, we were sometimes at odds, but you made it all happen, thank you. Chris Vranian, thank you for connecting me with Reel Art Press. Tony Nourmand, who said yes to publishing the book and has been a wonderful partner in its creation. Steve Jurgensmeyer for helping to conceptualize what a book might look like. A special thanks to all the Hip-Hop artists who participated in the film. Even if we were unable to include actual photos in this book, you gave of your time and trusted me to help tell the story of Hip-Hop during its Golden Age. For that I am eternally grateful.

To my parents Dorothy and Peter, who have always been supportive. And to my amazing and beautiful wife Kelly. The most together person I know. Always my anchor. I love you without measure.

THE BOOK OF
RHYME & REASON
PETER SPIRER

239
INDEX

Art Direction and Design: J A K E N O A K E S

Consultant: Soren Baker
Editor-in-Chief: Tony Nourmand
Managing Editor: Alison Elangasinghe
Pre-Press by HR Digital Solutions
With thanks to Dave Brolan

First published 2023 by Reel Art Press, an imprint of Rare Art Press Ltd, London, UK

reelartpress.com

First Edition
10 9 8 7 6 5 4 3 2 1

ISBN: 978-1-909526-89-1

All quotes from interviews conducted by Peter Spirer between 1994-1997 during the filming and production of *Rhyme & Reason*, except p.28, quote from DJ Kool Herc

Additional Captions:
p.200-1: Heavy D & His Crew; p. 210-11: Redman, Erick Sermon & Vin Rock (L-R)

Rhyme & Reason (1997) © Rhyme & Reason Inc/Miramax with permission

Printed in China